FRANCIS FRITH'S

DURHAM

PHOTOGRAPHIC MEMORIES

DEREK MACKENZIE-HOOK has been a travel writer for nearly twenty years. He now lives in the Scottish Borders and has fond memories of travels and family connections in the North East of England, particularly Durham. It was in 1996 that Derek first wrote about the progression of St Cuthbert from the historic Border town of Melrose where he began his ministry, to Holy Island where he was appointed Bishop of Lindisfarne. Amongst many other fascinating pieces of history, this book continues the journey of Cuthbert to his final resting place in Durham Cathedral.

FRANCIS FRITH'S
PHOTOGRAPHIC MEMORIES

DURHAM

PHOTOGRAPHIC MEMORIES

DEREK MACKENZIE-HOOK

First published in the United Kingdom in 2003 by
Frith Book Company Ltd

Limited Hardback Subscribers Edition Published in 2003
ISBN 1-85937-794-7

Paperback Edition 2003
ISBN 1-85937-499-9

British Library Cataloguing in Publication Data

Francis Frith's Durham - Photographic Memories
Derek Mackenzie-Hook
ISBN 1-85937-499-9

Frith Book Company Ltd
Frith's Barn, Teffont,
Salisbury, Wiltshire SP3 5QP
Tel: +44 (0) 1722 716 376
Email: info@francisfrith.co.uk
www.francisfrith.co.uk

Printed and bound in Great Britain

Front Cover: **DURHAM**, *The Cathedral 1892* 30735
Frontispiece: **DURHAM**, *The Cathedral 1923* 74079

*The colour-tinting is for illustrative purposes only, and is not intended to be
historically accurate*

AS WITH ANY HISTORICAL DATABASE THE FRITH ARCHIVE IS
CONSTANTLY BEING CORRECTED AND IMPROVED AND THE PUBLISHERS
WOULD WELCOME INFORMATION ON OMISSIONS OR INACCURACIES

CONTENTS

FRANCIS FRITH
VICTORIAN PIONEER

FRANCIS FRITH, founder of the world-famous photographic archive, was a complex and multi-talented man. A devout Quaker and a highly successful Victorian businessman, he was philosophic by nature and pioneering in outlook.

By 1855 he had already established a wholesale grocery business in Liverpool, and sold it for the astonishing sum of £200,000, which is the equivalent today of over £15,000,000. Now a very rich man, he was able to indulge his passion for travel. As a child he had pored over travel books written by early explorers, and his fancy and imagination had been stirred by family holidays to the sublime mountain regions of Wales and Scotland. 'What lands of spirit-stirring and enriching scenes and places!' he had written. He was to return to these scenes of grandeur in later years to 'recapture the thousands of vivid and tender memories', but with a different purpose. Now in his thirties, and captivated by the new science of photography, Frith set out on a series of pioneering journeys up the Nile and to the

Near East that occupied him from 1856 until 1860.

INTRIGUE AND EXPLORATION

These far-flung journeys were packed with intrigue and adventure. In his life story, written when he was sixty-three, Frith tells of being held captive by bandits, and of fighting 'an awful midnight battle to the very point of surrender with a deadly pack of hungry, wild dogs'. Wearing flowing Arab costume, Frith arrived at Akaba by camel seventy years before Lawrence of Arabia, where he encountered 'desert princes and rival sheikhs, blazing with jewel-hilted swords'.

He was the first photographer to venture beyond the sixth cataract of the Nile. Africa was still the mysterious 'Dark Continent', and Stanley and Livingstone's historic meeting was a decade into the future. The conditions for picture taking confound belief. He laboured for hours in his wicker dark-room in the sweltering heat of the desert, while the volatile chemicals fizzed dangerously in their trays. Back in London he exhibited his photographs and was 'rapturously cheered' by members of the Royal Society. His reputation as a photographer was made overnight.

VENTURE OF A LIFE-TIME

Characteristically, Frith quickly spotted the opportunity to create a new business as a specialist publisher of photographs. He lived in an era of immense and sometimes violent change.

For the poor in the early part of Victoria's reign work was exhausting and the hours long, and people had precious little free time to enjoy themselves. Most had no transport other than a cart or gig at their disposal, and rarely travelled far beyond the boundaries of their own town or village. However, by the 1870s the railways had threaded their way across the country, and Bank Holidays and half-day Saturdays had been made obligatory by Act of Parliament. All of a sudden the working man and his family were able to enjoy days out and see a little more of the world.

With typical business acumen, Francis Frith foresaw that these new tourists would enjoy having souvenirs to commemorate their days out. In 1860 he married Mary Ann Rosling and set out on a new career: his aim was to photograph every city, town and village in Britain. For the next thirty years he travelled the country by train and by pony and trap, producing fine photographs of seaside resorts and beauty spots that were keenly bought by millions of Victorians. These prints were painstakingly pasted into family albums and pored over during the dark nights of winter, rekindling precious memories of summer excursions.

THE RISE OF FRITH & CO

Frith's studio was soon supplying retail shops all over the country. To meet the demand he

gathered about him a small team of photographers, and published the work of independent artist-photographers of the calibre of Roger Fenton and Francis Bedford. In order to gain some understanding of the scale of Frith's business one only has to look at the catalogue issued by Frith & Co in 1886: it runs to some 670 pages, listing not only many thousands of views of the British Isles but also many photographs of most European countries, and China, Japan, the USA and Canada - note the sample page shown on page 9 from the hand-written Frith & Co ledgers recording the pictures. By 1890 Frith had created the greatest specialist photographic publishing company in the world, with over 2,000 sales outlets - more than the combined number that Boots and WH Smith have today! The picture on the next page shows the Frith & Co display board at Ingleton in the Yorkshire Dales (left of window). Beautifully constructed with a mahogany frame and gilt inserts, it could display up to a dozen local scenes.

POSTCARD BONANZA

The ever-popular holiday postcard we know today took many years to develop. In 1870 the Post Office issued the first plain cards, with a pre-printed stamp on one face. In 1894 they allowed other publishers' cards to be sent through the mail with an attached adhesive halfpenny stamp. Demand grew rapidly, and in 1895 a new size of postcard was permitted called the court card, but there was little room for illustration. In 1899, a year after Frith's death, a new card measuring 5.5 x 3.5 inches became the standard format, but it was not until 1902 that the divided back came into being, so that the address and message could be on one face and a full-size illustration on the other. Frith & Co were in the vanguard of postcard development: Frith's sons Eustace and Cyril continued their father's monumental task, expanding the number of views offered to the public and recording more and more places in

St Catherine's College
Senate House & Library
Gerrards Hostel Bridge
Geological Museum
Addenbrooke's Hospital
St Marys Church
Fitzwilliam Museum, Pitt Press &c
Buxton, The Crescent
The Colonnade
Public Gardens
Haddon Hall, View from the Terrace
Millers Dale

Britain, as the coasts and countryside were opened up to mass travel.

Francis Frith had died in 1898 at his villa in Cannes, his great project still growing. The archive he created continued in business for another seventy years. By 1970 it contained over a third of a million pictures showing 7,000 British towns and villages.

FRANCIS FRITH'S LEGACY

Frith's legacy to us today is of immense significance and value, for the magnificent archive of evocative photographs he created provides a unique record of change in the cities, towns and villages throughout Britain over a century and more. Frith and his fellow studio photographers revisited locations many times down the years to update their views, compiling for us an enthralling and colourful pageant of British life and character.

We are fortunate that Frith was dedicated to recording the minutiae of everyday life. For it is this sheer wealth of visual data, the painstaking chronicle of changes in dress, transport, street layouts, buildings, housing, engineering and landscape that captivates us so much today. His remarkable images offer us a powerful link with the past and with the lives of our ancestors.

THE VALUE OF THE ARCHIVE TODAY

Computers have now made it possible for Frith's many thousands of images to be accessed almost instantly. Frith's images are increasingly used as visual resources, by social historians, by researchers into genealogy and ancestry, by architects and town planners, and by teachers involved in local history projects.

In addition, the archive offers every one of us an opportunity to examine the places where we and our families have lived and worked down the years. Highly successful in Frith's own era, the archive is now, a century and more on, entering a new phase of popularity. Historians consider the Francis Frith Collection to be of prime national importance. It is the only archive of its kind remaining in private ownership. Francis Frith's archive is now housed in an historic timber barn in the beautiful village of Teffont in Wiltshire. Its founder would not recognize the archive office as it is today. In place of the many thousands of dusty boxes containing glass plate negatives and an all-pervading odour of photographic chemicals, there are now ranks of computer screens. He would be amazed to watch his images travelling round the world at unimaginable speeds through internet lines.

The archive's future is both bright and exciting. Francis Frith, with his unshakeable belief in making photographs available to the greatest number of people, would undoubtedly approve of what is being done today with his lifetime's work. His photographs depicting our shared past are now bringing pleasure and enlightenment to millions around the world a century and more after his death.

DURHAM
AN INTRODUCTION

DURHAM is a beautiful city that is both fascinating and interesting in myriad ways. Its cathedral, castle, university, ancient schools, bridges, churches, market place and array of public buildings are the principal threads woven into the colourful tapestry which is the city today. It is regarded as the historic capital of north-east England, as an important centre for culture and learning, and not least as an area of great natural beauty. Durham's special qualities were officially recognised by UNESCO in 1986 when its cathedral and castle were included in the first selection of World Heritage Sites, along with other universally-known places such as Stonehenge and the Taj Mahal.

The historic significance of Durham is inexorably linked with its being regarded as the cradle of Christianity in England. It was the resting place of the precious body of St Cuthbert, who died in 687; his remains were so venerated that when the Vikings sacked Lindisfarne, the monks left the island to seek a safe sanctuary for their relics. In 995, after years of wandering the north, the guardians of St Cuthbert's coffin came

St Hild's College 1903 50003

to a halt at a hill called Warden Law. Despite all the efforts of the monks, the cart carrying the coffin would not move any further, so their leader committed them to three days of fasting and prayer in order to learn the reason why the coffin would not move. Their prayers were finally answered when St Cuthbert appeared in a vision to a monk called Eadmer, and told him that the coffin should be taken to a place called Dun Holm. ('Dun' was an Anglo-Saxon word deriving from Celtic meaning 'hill', and 'holm', meaning 'island', is a word of Scandinavian origin). The monks discovered that they were now able to move the coffin and set off in search of this hill on an island. On their way they overheard a conversation between two milkmaids who were also on their way to Dun Holm to search for a lost dun-coloured cow, so they decided to follow them, and eventually reached their destination. Once the monks arrived on Dun Holm's rocky peninsula, they instantly decided that this would be an appropriate site for St Cuthbert's shrine.

Over the years the name has been simplified to the modern form - Durham. The legend of how Durham was first discovered is remembered in an 18th-century carving on the north wall of Durham Cathedral, which depicts the milk maid and her dun cow.

The high ground at Dun Holm, protected on three sides by the steep wooded gorge of the River Wear, provided an ideal, easily defended site for the resting place of St Cuthbert and other treasures from Lindisfarne Priory. His body first rested in a hastily erected church built from the boughs of trees and roofed with turf - this building is said to have occupied the site of the present church of St Mary-le-Bow. After the monks had cleared the thick woodland, a more substantial white-washed timber building, called the White Church, was erected. The wood also provided ideal building material for the first houses in the newly born city of Durham. The church was eventually replaced in 999 by the Anglo-Saxon minster, which was built of stone and also white-washed. This white church soon became a place of pilgrimage as miracles attributed to St Cuthbert became more and more well-known. The early cathedral and shrine was visited by hundreds of pilgrims who came to visit Durham in the same way as pilgrims had visited Lindisfarne a century before. Among the visitors was King Canute the Dane (1017-1035): as a mark of respect, he walked six miles to the site from Garmondsway, which is now a deserted medieval village situated near Coxhoe.

As well as being an important place of pilgrimage Durham was also an important defensive site. The ancient area called Northumbria, which included Durham, was a troublesome region that had to withstand many invasions from both the Vikings in the south and the Scots in the north. The Vikings had captured lands in southern Northumbria to form the great Viking kingdom centered upon York. However, it was the Scots who were to pose the greatest threat to the wealthy shrine of St Cuthbert for many years to come. The Scots made their first attack on the small city in 1006; fortunately they were quickly repelled, and many of the invaders lost their heads to an army of English comprised of Northumbrians and Yorkshiremen. The Scottish heads were displayed around Durham's city walls as a menacing warning against further attack. Four of the city's women were each presented with the generous gift of a cow for washing the heads and combing the hair of the best-looking Scots heads on display - nice work if you can get it!

William the Conqueror may have been aware of the earlier fatal defeat of the Scots, but he was not deterred in his aim to take control of the city. He is said to have visited Durham with the intention of viewing the uncorrupted body of St Cuthbert. He ordered his men to expose the body, and threatened to put to death all Durham churchmen of senior rank if it were found that the saint's body was not in an incorrupt state. But before the king had even looked at the saint's coffin, he found himself breathless and panic-stricken by a sudden burning fever. Thinking himself to be possessed by some strange force associated with St Cuthbert, he quickly fled from Durham and would not dismount his horse until he had crossed the River Tees into Yorkshire. The lane by which the king made his hasty retreat from Durham acquired the name of 'King's Ride', or Kingsgate, which in those days led to a ford across the River Wear. Today it is called Bow Lane, which leads across the River Wear by means of the Kingsgate footbridge.

The strategic importance of Durham became evident after the Norman invasion of Britain in 1066. The old Saxon defences were replaced, and a more sophisticated stronghold was built beside the minster in 1072 by William I to aid his ruthless suppression of the northern rebellion. Initially, the castle consisted of a timber stockade on an earthen mound, but by the end of the century the stronghold had been fortified and a bailey built around the level ground to the west. Shortly before his death, William I gave the castle to Bishop Walcher, the first of the Prince Bishops of Durham. William I, the Conqueror, was the first to recognise the value to the monarchy of a powerful bishopric in the north, and so the bishops were kings in all but name and held ecclesiastical and political sovereignty over the Palatinate of Durham. They had complete control, which meant having their own army, mint, and courts, and the right to levy taxes, create barons, grant charters for markets and fairs, and negotiate truces with the Scots.

The word 'bishopric' means 'the realm of the bishop', which in those days meant the area between the rivers Tyne and Tees - this later

Elvet Bridge 1918 68235

became known as the County Palatinate of Durham. These lands were intended to act as a buffer zone between England and Scotland; from here the warrior bishops' strong forces could act quickly to quell invaders from the north. William I knew that the Bishop of Durham would never contemplate joining forces with the Scots against his own sovereign, whereas a powerful secular noble might have done so had the terms been favourable.

It was not until the 18th and 19th centuries that the declining threat of constant invasion meant that life in Durham changed. This new-found stability prompted redevelopment on a scale not seen in the city for hundreds of years. It began to assume its modern character, and grand country and town houses were built for the landed gentry, the lawyers and the merchants. Many had prospered from exploiting coalfields beneath their land, but fortunately for Durham the seams beneath the city were not worth mining - otherwise many of the historic buildings could have been affected by subsidence. Although coalmines are now almost non-existent in County Durham, one of the biggest

events in the county today is the Miners' Gala, held in July. The event is but a shadow of its former self, but for decades it was the focal point of the year for every miner and his family. At its height, prior to the First World War, the event was the largest annual gathering by the working classes in Britain, with crowds often in excess of 100,000. During the 1925 Gala, the year before the General Strike, the dean of Durham was thrown into the River Wear by miners who had mistaken him for the bishop – the bishop had unwisely expressed the view that miners did not deserve an increase in pay. Many great speakers from the Labour movement attended the Gala, including: Clement Attlee, Ernest Bevin, Aneurin Bevan, Harold Wilson, Michael Foot and Tony Benn. Although still recognised as one of the last great miners' gatherings, the Durham Miners' Gala today is more of a festival with a varied programme of entertainment; it continues to be one of the highlights of the county's social calendar.

More and more industries began to establish themselves in Durham, such as a mustard mill and a woollen mill – this was later converted into a successful carpet factory. Organ building was

The Cathedral Choir, East 1892 30745

another important local industry, and the firm Harrison & Harrison, founded in 1861 and one of the most famous organ builders in Britain, still exists today. The company's work included the organs for many cathedrals, including Ely, Winchester, Worcester and Durham itself. Other notable organs include the ones at Westminster Abbey, York Minster and the Royal Albert Hall.

The city itself has continued to develop within the limits determined by the course of the river, which has virtually dictated the limits of development in the historic area and the pattern of its narrow winding streets. In 1724, Daniel Defoe said of the city:

'The city of Durham appears like a confused heap of stones and brick, accumulated so as to cover a mountain, round which a river winds its brawling course. The streets are generally narrow, dark and unpleasant, and many of them impassable in consequence of their declivity'.

It was not until the completion of the new inner through road in the early 1970s that all traffic moving across the city could avoid passing through the Market Place. Durham today still has a remarkable variety of streets and buildings of all ages. It has managed to retain much of its original character, and there has been little change to the basic structure of some of the oldest buildings. A 14th-century monk would have no difficulty in recognising some of buildings portrayed in the photographs in this book. However, many of the older buildings associated with industrial development have now been demolished, and the accompanying increase in population has seen the modern city grow outwards. Today Durham has a population of about 80,000, compared with about 2000 in 1635. It serves the county through its administrative offices and modern shopping facilities, and there is a thriving community centred on the university. Durham is the only county in England that is prefixed with the word County, as in Ireland. This is partly a remnant of the days when County Durham was termed the County Palatine of Durham, the realm of the prince bishops, and partly to distinguish it from Durham the city.

The photographs in this book give an insight into historical events in the 10th century; they also show how this vibrant city has retained so much of its historical interest.

Old Elvet 1914 67127

THE CATHEDRAL

The Cathedral 1892 30741
From whichever direction we approach the city, Durham Cathedral dominates the landscape. The sheer size of this magnificent structure is awesome: the central tower soars to a phenomenal 218ft and has 325 steps, should we wish to tackle the ascent. The entire building stretches 470ft from the east wall of the Chapel of the Nine Altars to the west wall of the Galilee Chapel, and the great nave runs for 201ft, its roof vault rising some 72ft.

The Cathedral 1892
30742

The work of building the cathedral can be attributed to several distinct periods. The nave, transepts and the four west choir bays were built between 1093 and 1133; Bishop Hugh Pudsey added the Galilee Chapel at the western end in 1175; the two west towers were built between 1217 and 1226; then the east end of the choir was altered and the Chapel of the Nine Altars erected between 1242 and 1280. The great central tower was rebuilt between 1465 and 1495 after lightning and fire had destroyed its predecessor some 60 years earlier.

17

▲ *The Cathedral 1918* 68213

The long, battlemented single-storey building immediately in front of the west towers is the Galilee Chapel, built by Bishop Hugh Le Puiset, who was known more affectionately as Bishop Pudsey (1153-1195). The Galilee is also the cathedral's Lady Chapel. These chapels are normally constructed at the eastern end of cathedrals, and not at the west. Initially there had been an attempt to build the Lady Chapel at the eastern end, but the foundations were insecure and the walls began to crack. This was taken as a sign that St Cuthbert disliked the idea of a Lady Chapel near to his tomb, so the chapel was constructed at the west end. However, at a later stage another chapel, the Chapel of the Nine Altars, was built at the cathedral's east end – mysteriously, this seems to have had no major structural problems.

▶

The Cathedral, the Galilee 1892 30753

The Galilee Chapel is also the Lady Chapel; it was once the only part of the cathedral that could be entered by women, according to the rules of the Benedictine order of monks. A little way inside the main cathedral building there is a line of black marble in the cathedral floor, which marked the point beyond which women were not allowed to pass. Also here is Bede's tomb. The manuscript of Bede's *Life of Cuthbert* epitomises the connection between the goodness of Cuthbert and the learning of the Venerable Bede, who is responsible for everything we know about Cuthbert. He was also influential in bringing about the way of reckoning years that gave us BC, 'before Christ', and AD, 'Anno Domini', Latin for 'in the year of our Lord.' His works include *The History of the English Church and People*, one of the main sources for the history of this period.

The Cathedral through the Trees 1892 30732

When William the Conqueror finally took control of Durham, he combined the powers of the bishop and the Earl of Northumbria to create Durham's first prince bishop, a Norman called William Walcher. Walcher's leadership was weak, which ultimately resulted in his being murdered at Gateshead in 1081. His replacement was William St Carileph, the man responsible for building the present cathedral, which occupies the site of the old stone minster built by Uchted. Carileph began its construction in 1093. He designed the greater part of the cathedral as it stands today; the new building was completed to the bishop's designs in around forty years. Unfortunately, Carileph did not live to see the completion of his cathedral in 1135.

The Cathedral from the River 1892 30730

The River Wear has been vital to Durham through the centuries - its great loop creates the city's natural defence. Below the towering cathedral are the beautiful woodlands, still threaded with a maze of footpaths that criss-cross the river.

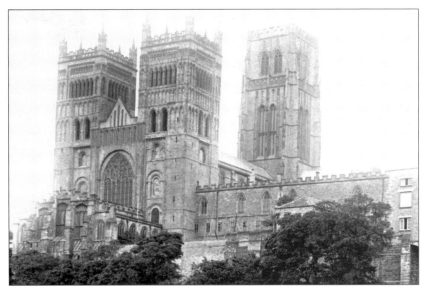

The Cathedral 1892 30734

The picturesque building below the cathedral (see 30730, above) is the old fulling mill, standing beside its weir. Once the property of the priors of Durham, the fulling mill was once known as the Jesus Mill; it now houses the Durham University Museum of Archaeology. The mill dates from the start of the 15th century, when it played its part in the growing weaving trade at that time. During the 1950s it was a popular riverside café. Then it was converted into the present-day museum, where exhibits illustrate the early history of Durham and the surrounding area.

The Cathedral from the River 1921 70712

Once a vital part of the city's defences, the river in recent times
has been used for more pleasurable purposes. Boating is a
popular pastime, and the river is used by a variety of pleasure
and competitive craft. In the foreground we see a couple of
moored rowing boats that would be used to take lady friends for a
gentle meander along the river on a fine, sunny afternoon,
whereas on the river are a couple of skiffs that would be used for
more competitive purposes.

The Cathedral North Side c1883 16143

After climbing through the narrow streets of Durham, we suddenly come upon a dramatic opening into the light and space of Palace Green, dominated by the awesome cathedral. This great space was created by Bishop Flambard at the beginning of the 12th century: he decided to demolish the clutter of wooden houses and the market place because of the potential fire hazard to the castle and cathedral.

The Cathedral c1955 D71036

Palace Green is a large, well-tended area between the castle and the cathedral, enclosed on both sides by a range of historic buildings dating from the 18th century. Most of these belong to the university, and include the former Grammar School, located near the cathedral towers. This building is reputedly haunted by a young pupil who was allegedly thrown from a balcony by one of his masters in a fit of anger.

The New Lecture Rooms Palace Green 1929
82399

The Tudor-style building on the right of the photograph, the Pemberton Building, houses the new lecture rooms, which were opened in 1931.

▶ *The Cathedral
the North Door 1923* 74081

The great north door was made in the
12th century, and is the main
entrance to the cathedral. Bishop
Pudsey created the north porch in the
1150s, and it was then that the door's
famous sanctuary knocker (see
photograph No 9434) was fitted.
There was once a small room above
the north porch where two monks
would keep vigil day and night,
watching for fugitives seeking
sanctuary. Note the iron outer gates:
these were fitted after it was
discovered in 1915 that the northern
suffragettes were planning to damage
one of the pillars in the nave to gain
publicity for their cause. A local
suffragette did not support the idea
and gave a word of warning, so the
iron grille was fitted as a precaution.

▶ *The Cathedral
Crypt c1862* 1119

Photograph 1119 is
the earliest in this
book. The crypt is one
of the oldest parts of
the cathedral, and is
now used to house the
Treasures of St
Cuthbert exhibition
and the cathedral
restaurant. Most
visitors to the
cathedral use the
cloisters to gain
access to the
restaurant, the
bookshop and the
Treasury Museum,
one of the most
important museums
in the north of
England.

▶ *The Cathedral
the North Door, the Sanctuary Knocker c1877* 9434

The grimacing face of the sanctuary knocker is hardly a welcoming
sight for visitors or those seeking refuge in the cathedral. It
represents the right of sanctuary for fugitives, who could find
temporary shelter in the cathedral from their pursuers. The right of
sanctuary can be traced back to 597. Later Saxon laws gave these
special privileges to St Cuthbert's community in around 900.
The Normans continued to observe the tradition, and at Durham
sanctuary was granted for 37 days. The Galilee bell was tolled to
inform everyone that a fugitive was present; he would only be
admitted if he had no weapons. He would be given food and drink
and made to wear a black gown with a large yellow cross of St
Cuthbert on the left shoulder. In fact, it was not really necessary for
the pursued to enter the cathedral, because the boundaries of
sanctuary at Durham probably extended as far as Neville's Cross and
Gilesgate. A replica knocker now replaces the original, which can be
seen in the Treasures of St Cuthbert exhibition in the cathedral.

◄ *The Cathedral Crypt 1921* 70723

▶ *The Cathedral, Nave and Screen c1877* 9418

The 900-year-old nave measures 61m long, 12m wide and 22m high. Its massive columns support the impressive stone-ribbed vaulted roof, the earliest example of rib vaulting in Europe. This structural innovation was of enormous significance, as it became a widely used feature in later Gothic cathedrals. The magnificent Neville screen was a gift from the Neville family in celebration of the victory against the Scots at the battle of Neville's Cross in 1346. In honour of his victory, Ralph Neville became the first layman to be allowed burial in the cathedral. Behind the screen is the tomb of St Cuthbert. A wooden plaque bears the following inscription: 'Borne by his faithful friends from his loved home of Lindisfarne, here, after long wanderings, rests the body of St Cuthbert in whose honour William of St Carileph built this cathedral church, and at his side lies buried the head of St Oswald King of Northumbria and martyr, slain in battle by the heathen whom he so long defied'.

◀ *The Cathedral, Nave and Font 1921* 70716

The magnificent font canopy was designed for Bishop Cosin by James Clement, a Durham architect, and installed in 1663. The octagonal canopy is over 12m high, and its ornate decoration emphasises the significance of baptism in the life of the church. The huge marble font used today also dates from the time of John Cosin, who was a canon at Durham during the reign of Charles I, and later bishop under Charles II. However, the font in the photograph is a mock Norman font that was installed in 1846 to replace the original, which was then deemed to be 'unsuitable' - it was 1935 before the Cosin font was returned to its rightful place.

▲ *The Cathedral, the Choir looking East 1892* 30745

The medieval stone screen dividing the nave from the choir was demolished some time in the 16th century and replaced in about 1665 by one of richly carved wood. This new screen, together with the choir stalls which also date from 1665, are said to have been designed for Bishop Cosin by James Clement, who was also responsible for the carved font canopy in the nave (see photograph 70716). The original choir stalls and font canopy had been burnt by Scots prisoners imprisoned in the cathedral after the battle of Dunbar in 1650. At the far end of the choir is the high altar. Above it is the magnificent rose window, over 98ft (30m) in circumference. It shows Christ, 'the Saviour of the World', as the inscription says, surrounded by the twelve apostles and the twenty-four elders from the Book of Revelation.

▶ *The Cathedral, the Bishop's Throne 1925* 77669

This impressive bishop's throne is said to be the highest in Christendom. Below the throne is the tomb of Bishop Thomas Hatfield, who is reputed to have decided that the bishops of Durham deserved a throne equal in height to that of the Bishop of Rome – the Pope!

▶ *The Cathedral,
the Memorial Chapel 1925*
77671

The Memorial Chapel was dedicated in
1924 to commemorate Durham's own
regiment, the Durham Light Infantry. It
contains the regimental colours and
books of remembrance listing the
names of those who fell in battle.

▼ *The Cathedral
Library c1877* 9440

The cathedral library is housed in the
former monks' dormitory above the
western walkway of the cloisters. It
dates from the 14th century. The
picture shows the impressive roof of
oak beams, which looks like the hull of
an upturned wooden ship. The library
now belongs to the dean and chapter,
and houses a collection of Anglo-Saxon
and Viking crosses from throughout the
ancient kingdom of Northumbria.

THE CASTLE

The Castle 1921 70724

The city of Durham is still dominated from all viewpoints by the castle and the cathedral. Founded in 1072, Durham Castle is one of the largest Norman castles and one of the grandest Romanesque palaces to survive in England. It was built on the site of a fortress to the orders of William the Conqueror on his return from Scotland in 1072, sited on a peninsular overlooking the River Wear and positioned next to a Benedictine monastery. Waltheof, the Saxon Earl of Northumberland, undertook the building work, but over the years a succession of prince bishops have added important sections to the great building. In the 1930s a huge rescue operation had to be carried out to underpin the subsiding foundations: while the cathedral was built on solid bedrock, the castle was built on less substantial material. Together with the cathedral, the castle is now a World Heritage Site.

The Castle
c1955 D71035

This gatehouse near the castle moat is the main entrance to the castle and its courtyard. The gatehouse is primarily the work of Bishop Pudsey (1153-1195), but it underwent alterations during the episcopacies of Bishop Tunstall (1530-1559) and Bishop Shute Barrington (1791-1826). Evidence of Norman work is still visible in the outer arch of the gateway, and the passage within has a medieval vaulted roof. The great gates themselves are believed to date back to the early 16th century. However, the outer walls and upper floors of the gatehouse were rebuilt in 'Gothick' style by the fashionable architect James Wyatt for Bishop Barrington (1791-1826) at the end of the 18th century.

► *The Castle Courtyard 1918* 68215

To the right of the gatehouse is a curtain wall; behind it is the Fellows' private garden. Next to this is a three-storey building called Garden Stairs, which now houses various administrative and domestic offices. It carries over its doorway the arms of Bishop Cosin (1660-1672), who was responsible for the restoration of the building in the late 17th century, although parts of it date from a much earlier period. Next to this is the Great Hall, built in the 13th and 14th centuries by Bishop Bek (1284-1310) and Bishop Hatfield (1345-1381). Under Hatfield's design, the Hall proper occupied the whole of this large block, but the area to the left of the main door was converted to four storeys of rooms at the end of the 15th century. The entrance porch, with matched pairs of Ionic columns on each side, was added by Bishop Cosin, whose coat of arms is on the wall above.

◄ *The Castle Dining Hall 1921* 70726

The Great Hall of the castle is now the dining hall of University College, and compares very well with those of Oxford and Cambridge colleges. It is one of the largest and most impressive of its kind in the country, and the timber roof dates to the time of Bishop Hatfield (1345-1381). Many English monarchs have been entertained here over the centuries. Much of the hall's interior, however, goes back no further than the foundation of the University in the 1830s; the oak panelling and the entrance screen were inserted shortly after 1882 to commemorate the University's fiftieth anniversary. Housed in the Great Hall are a variety of military trophies, including a set of Cromwellian helmets and breastplates and an array of rifles and flags from the Napoleonic wars.

▲ *The Castle 1892* 30759

The irregularly shaped courtyard corresponds to the inner bailey of the original Norman fortress.
The mixture of architectural styles and the work of individual bishops can be identified by the coats
of arms which are placed in conspicuous places on the walls. The arms of Bishop Cosin appear on
the wall of the great tower of the Black Staircase (see 30763, page 36) which juts into the courtyard to
the right of the Great Hall. The building to the right is the late 12th-century building of Bishop
Pudsey (1153-1195). The upper part was restored in the 18th century by Bishop Trevor, whose arms
are set high on the wall, and the original Norman windows took on their present shape then. Below
is the Gallery, built in the first half of the 16th century by Bishop Tunstall to link the Great Hall with
his bell-tower and chapel - his arms are on the lower wall of the tower and Gallery. Note the bowler-
hatted gardener carefully tending the lawns. In those days there would have been a head gardener
with a squad of probably fifty or more assistants to maintain the gardens and grounds.

◄ *The Castle 1918* 68216

Tunstall's chapel, in the north-east
corner of the courtyard, was extended
to the east under Bishops Cosin and
Crewe at the end of the 17th century.
Next to this is the impressive castle
keep; although it is the most imposing
part of the castle, it is in fact the least
ancient. Only the chapel and part of
the undercroft of the great hall survive
to this day, but the layout of the keep
and courtyard follows the original
pattern. In the tradition of the
Norman motte and bailey castles, the
keep is situated on a mound. Over the
centuries the keep fell into a ruinous
state, but it was rebuilt in the 1840s to
be used as sleeping quarters for
students when the castle became
Durham's University College.

▶ *The Castle,*
the Black Staircase 1892 30763

This is Bishop Cosin's impressive Black Staircase; it stands in the angled tower between the Great Hall and the 12th-century building of Bishop Pudsey. Built in the early 1660s, the Black Staircase is one of the most impressive staircases of its time in the country. It is 17m high, and with the exception of the intricately carved softwood side panels, is made from oak.

▼ *The Castle,*
Tunstall's Gallery 1918 68218

From the first landing of the Black Staircase leads Bishop Tunstall's gallery. The inner wall of this gallery was formerly the outer wall of Bishop Pudsey's hall, and the great round-headed doorway (see 30762) which faces the gallery's largest window was once the principal entrance to the lower part of this 12th-century building.

The Castle, the Norman Arch 1892 30762

This great round-headed doorway was once the principal entrance to the lower part of the 12th-century building that stands directly opposite the castle gatehouse, and was probably approached under a canopy by a long flight of steps from the courtyard. The doorway is in near immaculate condition, and is generally reckoned to be one of the finest examples of late Romanesque stone carving in England.

SCHOOLS AND COLLEGES

Durham School 1929 82407

Durham is also famous for its public school, which probably existed before the time of William the Conqueror. The most expensive public school in the north-east boasts many famous pupils, including the novelist Robert Smith Surtees (1803-64), creator of the characters Jorrocks and Mr Soapy Sponge. The school building was adapted from an existing house, and moved to its present site in 1844. Further additions were made between 1853 and the present day.

Durham School
the Kerr Memorial and
the School Chapel 1929
82408

The inscription over the arched gate reads: 'In grateful memory of Graham Campbell Kerr, a loyal son of the school, born 1872, sn 1886-1890, Assistant Master 1895-1901, Governor of the Red Sea Province, Sudan 1909, died August 18th 1913.' The building on the hill beyond the school gate is the chapel, which was erected as a war memorial in 1924-26.

Bede College 1929 82403

The impressive College of the Venerable Bede was founded in 1839 as a Church of England college to train young men as schoolteachers. St Bede's College closed in 1975, and was amalgamated with St Hild's in 1979.

▲ *St Hild's College 1903* 50003

A diocesan training school for schoolmistresses, St Hild's College was founded in 1858 alongside its male counterpart, St Bede's. The colleges of St Hild and St Bede have a long and distinguished individual history, but in 1979 they combined to become a full member of the university. Today the college of St Hild and St Bede is the largest of the Durham colleges with over a thousand students, of which nearly six hundred live in the college's accommodation.

◀ *Hatfield College 1923* 74100

Hatfield College was founded in 1846, and is the second oldest college in Durham. It was named after the 14th-century Bishop Thomas Hatfield, and opened for the specific purpose of providing a residence for young men who could not afford to live in University College. Hatfield's students were provided with furnished rooms and meals that were taken communally, unlike their well-heeled counterparts at Durham School.

▶ *Neville's Cross College 1923*
74094

Neville's Cross College was founded in 1921, originally to be specifically for County Durham girls. In the early days the college was often disparagingly referred to by locals as 'that jam factory on the hill.' The college has been extended over the years; it is now New College, a college for further education.

◀ *Neville's Cross College the Dining Room 1923* 74098

The facilities at Neville's Cross were far in advance of those at many other colleges built at that time. Students here had the luxury of their own rooms rather than dormitories, and a grand dining hall in which students and staff all dined together.

▲ *St Chad's College 1923* 74080

The entrance to St Chad's is the arched opening on the right. This is located just 50m from the cathedral; it fronts onto the Bailey, a mediaeval street that follows the spine of the peninsula from the historic Market Place to Prebends Bridge.

◄ *St Chad's College Gateway 1923* 74083

St Chad's College, the smallest of the Durham colleges, was licensed in 1904 by the Durham University Senate as the first independent hall of the university. However, following a reappraisal of the college's status, the college ceased training people for the priesthood in 1971.

St Chad's position as a college of the university was unaffected, and it has since accepted men and women to read for all university degrees.

Ushaw Moor
Ushaw College c1960
U17009

The famous Roman Catholic seminary of Ushaw College is the main centre in the north of England for the training of Roman Catholic priests. Its establishment dates back to the foundation of the great seminary at Douai in France, which was founded in 1568 to supply Catholic missionaries to England during a period of Catholic repression. The college is the home of St Cuthbert's finger ring, which may be worn by the Roman Catholic Bishop of Hexham and Newcastle on special occasions.

BUILDINGS
AND STREETS

The Shire Hall 1921 70730

The old Shire Hall was built between 1895-98 and enlarged in 1905. Despite the fact that this essentially red brick building was once described as a 'grotesque monstrosity', there is much to admire. Its copper-coloured dome is something of a landmark, and the Weardale marble, together with stained glass from Glasgow, contribute to the building's quality. Since 1963, when Durham County Council moved its headquarters away from the Shire Hall, it has been the administrative centre of Durham University.

The Town Hall, Interior 1918 68231

The old Town Hall, known as the Guildhall, was built in 1356, and many alterations were made right up to the middle of the 18th century. The Guildhall has connections with the old city guilds, some of which still exist and meet here. The main function of the medieval guilds was to oversee and guarantee high standards of workmanship and to ensure a monopoly for their members. By the middle of the 19th century, the Guildhall had ceased to be a suitable building to accommodate the business of the growing city, so in 1850 a new town hall was built behind the old structure. The new hall was designed to be a smaller-scale version of Westminster Hall - our photograph shows the impressive hammer-beam roof. Other interesting features include superb stained-glass windows, paintings and heraldic symbols, and a magnificent fireplace of local Prudhoe stone

Market Place c1915 D71301

This wonderful photograph shows a beautiful convertible car, probably belonging to one of the landed gentry; the two delivery men enjoy a break whilst their horses tuck into their nosebags; and the little boy watches the cameraman at work. The spire of St Nicholas's dominates the Market Place. In 1857 this Victorian church replaced an earlier church of St Nicholas, which dated from the 12th century - it had a tower. On the left, next to the Prudential Assurance building, is the Market Tavern, where the Miners Union was formed in 1871. In the foreground is the statue of Neptune on top of the octagonal pant (a northern word for a public fountain). Neptune was placed here in 1729 to symbolise an ambitious plan to turn Durham into an inland sea port; this would have resulted in the unthinkable - the joining of the rivers Tyne and Wear! Neptune's neighbour is the statue of the 3rd Marquess of Londonderry, who owned collieries around Durham and also constructed Seaham Harbour in 1828. The statue was sculpted by Raphael Monti, who reputedly committed suicide following the discovery of a flaw in his creation. According to legend, Monti had boasted that his statue was perfect, but a blind beggar man was feeling in the mouth of the horse and discovered that it had no tongue.

Market Place c1955 D71054

This is a photograph of the busy Market Place with lots of cars, no horses and no Neptune! The pant was demolished in 1923, and Neptune was moved to a life of solitude in Wharton Park. Fortunately, he was returned to his rightful place in the Market Square in 1991. The Prudential Assurance building and Market Tavern are still evident, but note the modern building on the right of Londonderry's statue. The Market Place today is virtually a pedestrian precinct. There is no longer a policeman sitting in a peculiar box controlling the traffic from the Market Place with a closed-circuit television monitor (bottom right), and drivers now have to pay a charge to drive through the square into Saddler Street.

Silver Street c1955 D71024

Silver Street is typical of the narrow winding streets that lead to
the focal point of the city, the Market Square. It is said to have
acquired its name from once being the site of a mint where
unique Durham coins were produced. Traffic no longer
negotiates this steep curving street, for today only pedestrians are
permitted to explore this ancient way. One of the busiest
shopping streets in the city, it is now dominated by modern shop
fronts catering for students and the tourist trade, but its
narrowness is a constant reminder of its medieval origins.

Old Elvet 1914 67127

This area was once the site of the city's horse fair. The street is unusually wide and spacious for Durham; it was further extended in the 1960s, when road development saw the demise of the Waterloo Hotel, the building beyond the Royal County Hotel (right). The fountain of 1863 in the centre of the photograph disappeared before the Second World War. The Royal County Hotel is noted for its balcony, on which prominent leaders of the Labour Party and mineworkers acknowledge the parades on Miners' Gala Day. Inside, the hotel is notable for its impressive black staircase dating from 1660, which is said to have been brought here from Loch Leven Castle in Scotland. Students formerly referred to Old Elvet as Three Taverns because of its trinity of locations to sup their ale.

The Cathedral and the Old Tithe Barn, Hallgarth 1929 82398

The timber-framed building in the foreground was part of a small group of medieval buildings that once belonged to the prior's manor of Elvet. The old tithe barn and the building on its right have been renovated and are now Crown property. The barn now houses the Prison Officers' Club, which must be one of the most unusual uses ever found for a medieval building.

Durham, North Road c1955 D71059

This busy shopping area in North Road was formerly known as King Street, so named because it was opened in 1831, the year of William IV's coronation. Following redevelopment to accommodate increased traffic using the Great North Road, the Mill Burn was diverted into a culvert under North Road, the land was drained and houses on Framwellgate Bridge were demolished to make way for a new improved road north. The upper part of this was called North Road, and the lower end we see here, King Street.

The Count's House 1914 67129

The Count's House is associated with a Polish-born count called Joseph Boruwlaski; he was remarkable for many reasons, including the fact that he was only 39in tall. Often referred to as the Polish Dwarf or Little Count, he was an accomplished violinist whose musical talent earned him many notable friends and admirers, including George IV and Marie Antoinette. He died at the grand age of 97, and having established himself as a respected member of Durham society, was buried in the cathedral, where his grave is simply marked 'JB'. Although it is still referred to as the Count's House, this little garden house of the 1820s, built in the style of a Greek Doric temple on the banks of the Wear, is actually a folly built near the site of his home. Sad to say, the Count's House today is just a neglected ruin; its association with a diminutive man who was larger than life in the city's history is now apparently forgotten.

Prebend's Cottage 1914 67128

This quaint little cottage still nestles on the roadside leading from Prebends Bridge. The road is closed to traffic, but it is a popular route across the river for students of Durham School, the oldest public school in the country.

From Pelaw Wood 1918 68234

The view across the river from the wooded slopes of Pelaw Wood is
magnificent. In the distance are the cathedral and the castle, and
below is the former race course alongside the river. The woods were
given to the City of Durham by Lord Londonderry earlier last century.

The Race Course 1918 68232

This photograph shows the former horse-racing track on the right
and Pelaw Woods in the distance. The race course, formerly known
as Smiddyhaughs, meaning 'the riverside fields belonging to the
smith', was closed in 1887, and is now the university playing fields.
We can see from the amount of people both on the river and along
the banks how popular this area is. One of the delights of this fine
city even today is that within minutes we can be away from the
hustle and bustle in its crowded streets and enjoying the gentle
ambience of the River Wear.

BRIDGES

Prebends Bridge 1892 30756

Built in 1777, Prebends Bridge (so-called because only the prebends or canons of the cathedral have the right to drive a vehicle across it) probably offers the most spectacular views of the cathedral. Turner painted the Durham peninsula from here, and at the bridge's west end is a plaque bearing an extract from Sir Walter Scott's poem on Durham: *'Grey Towers of Durham Yet well I love thy mixed and varied piles, Half church of God, half castle 'gainst the Scot, And long to roam these venerable aisles With records stored of deeds long since forgot.'* At the east end are two sculptures by Colin Wilbourn, former artist in residence at Durham Cathedral.
The building in the background is the boathouse for Durham School Rowing Club.

Prebends Bridge and the River Bank 1914 67132

We are looking in the opposite direction to 30756; this view was
taken from the boathouse of Durham School Rowing Club. The bend
in the river beyond the bridge is known as Count's Corner, so called
because the Count's House is located here (see 67129, page 53).

Framwellgate Bridge 1892 30739

Dating from around 1120, the bridge was built as part of the relocation of townsfolk to Crossgate following the clearance of dwellings to create the Palace Green. Only a small part of the original bridge remains after being severely damaged by flooding. It was rebuilt in 1401; the tower and gateway on the bridge were demolished in 1760. The bridge was widened in the 19th century, but for 800 years, up until the 1970s when a new through road was built, this bridge and the narrow Silver Street (see D71024, page 49), had to carry all the city centre traffic, including buses and lorries. The bridge has witnessed many notable events over the years, including the murder in 1318 of the bishop's steward Richard Fitzmarmaduke by his cousin Ralph Neville, 'the Peacock of the North.'

Elvet Bridge 1918 68235

Dating originally from the episcopacy of Hugh du Puiset (1153-1195), Elvet Bridge has been frequently repaired and altered over the centuries. The bridge was reconstructed in 1228; further repairs were required in 1500, and again in 1771 after three of the arches were destroyed by the great flood. The houses were cleared from the north side in 1790, and in 1805 the bridge's width was doubled. The building on the right with the Dutch gable is actually sitting on the bridge above a dry arch. It is situated on the Elvet side of the bridge on the site of the medieval chapel of St Andrew, which was built between 1274 and 1283. Elvet Bridge is one of only three bridges in England that have houses built on them.

Elvet Bridge 1918 68236

This excellent view shows six of the bridge's ten arches, four of which are on dry land - two of these are obscured by buildings. In medieval times a number of buildings were built on this bridge, including the chapels of St Andrew and St James which stood at either end. The latter was replaced by the House of Correction in 1632; this was the former home of Jamie Allan. A celebrated Northumbrian piper and sometime villain, it is reputed that the strains of Allan's pipes are still to be heard around Elvet Bridge. Near the bridge is Brown's boathouse, where boats can be rented. Brown's is noted for building racing fours and eights, and many of the local oarsmen use these to participate in the Durham Regatta (see 70712 page 21). The numbers on the bridge piers are for competitors in the regatta, England's second oldest and held each June since 1836.

CHURCHES

St Oswald's Church 1918 68226

The earliest part of this church dates from the 12th century, but the site is thought to be older, as a number of Anglo-Saxon finds have been made. The church is dedicated to St Oswald, the Christian Northumberland monarch who died in 642 and whose skull is interred in Cuthbert's tomb.

St Mary the Less Church 1918 68227

This church was originally one of the smallest parish churches in England, built in the 12th century by one of the mighty Nevilles of Brancepeth Castle. The church was built as a place of worship for the retainers and fighting men who came to staff the city walls; since 1919 it has been the college chapel for St John's, one of the smallest university colleges. In the church is a memorial to Joseph Boruwlaski, the Polish dwarf. Although he was buried in the cathedral, his memorial was erected here because the wording on it was considered to be inappropriate to the great church.

St Giles' Church 1918 68228

St Giles' church is reputed to be the second oldest church in the city after the cathedral. The long, steeply banked street of Gilesgate is still occasionally known by its medieval name of Gillygate, meaning the street of St Giles.

▶ *St Margaret's Church 1918* 68229

St Margaret's church sits at the bottom of Crossgate, the ancient route west from the city, on a bluff overlooking Framwellgate Bridge. The interior retains some of the original 12th-century features, notably the four Norman arches in the south arcade.

◀ *St Mary-le-Bow 1918* 68230

St Mary-le-Bow is said to have been built on the site of the shelter (the Church of Boughs) which first housed the body of St Cuthbert. The church is now a Heritage Centre, Durham City's only local history museum, telling the story of Durham from medieval times to the present day. On display is the 'death chair', a sedan chair given to the Heritage Centre by Durham School, where it was used in the 19th century to carry sick boys to the sanatorium. It became known as the death chair because boys ill enough to be carried rarely returned.

▶ *St Cuthbert's Church c1883* 16160

This church was built in 1863, and was modelled on a church in Normandy. The tower of St Cuthbert's is a noted landmark in Durham, but it is in a somewhat perilous state - the soft stonework has suffered from erosion for the last 140 years.

◀ *St Godric's Church, the Interior c1883* 16158

The history of St Godric's begins in the late 1850s, when money was raised to buy land upon which to build a church. The new church was opened in 1864.

OTHER PLACES OF INTEREST

FINCHALE PRIORY *1892* 30724

In about 1104, Finchale became the site of a hermitage belonging to St Godric, who lived there for sixty years until he was 105. This 13th-century Benedictine priory was built around his burial-place; it is one of the most historic sites in the district of Durham City. The priory was used as a holiday retreat by monks in the 14th century. Finchale is mentioned as early as AD792, when it was the site of a synod for the Northumbrian church held to discuss church discipline.

FINCHALE PRIORY *1892* 30725

Following Godric's death, Finchale passed into the hands of
the priors of Durham Cathedral. A Benedictine priory was built
here around 1196 by Henry Pudsey, son of Hugh, Bishop of
Durham. From the 14th century the priory had four resident
monks, but monks from Durham Cathedral made regular visits
to Finchale, which they used as a kind of holiday retreat. It is
most likely that the monks travelled to Finchale above ground,
but there is a legend that a secret passage runs underground
from Durham Castle to Finchale.

▼ BRANCEPETH, *The Castle 1914* 67122

A lot of history revolves around Brancepeth Castle, which in spite of modern restorations has a long story to tell. The castle was owned by the mighty Neville family until the 16th century, when in 1569 it was confiscated by the Crown following their involvement in the Rising of the North and a plot to overthrow Queen Elizabeth I. Brancepeth was later bought in 1796 by William Russell, a Sunderland banker. The Russells of Brancepeth became one of four great coal mining families in the north who were known as the `Grand Allies'; William's son Matthew became the richest commoner in England. It was he who began the rebuilding of Brancepeth in 1817.

▶ BRANCEPETH
The Castle 1892 30722

It was in Brancepeth Castle that the rebel earls of Northumberland and Westmorland plotted their attack on Barnard Castle in 1569. At the time Barnard was being held by Sir George Bowes for Queen Elizabeth, and the rebellion collapsed after the earls were defeated near Durham.

BRANCEPETH
The Village 1914 67121

Of all the villages that surround Durham City, old Brancepeth is particularly well steeped in legend and history. The area caught the attention of both William Wordsworth, who visited the village and featured it in a poem, and Alfred Lord Tennyson, who wrote *Come into the Garden, Maud* at Brancepeth. At the end of the broad drive leading to the castle grounds are the fine entrance gates, beyond which is the 12th-century church of St Brandon. Inside the church was the 17th-century woodwork associated with Bishop John Cosin (1660-1672) and the effigy of Robert Neville, who was known as the 'Peacock of the North.' Unfortunately the church and its contents were badly damaged by fire in 1998.

BISHOP AUCKLAND
The Castle 1892 30706

Auckland Castle, also known as Auckland Palace, began as a manor house built in about 1183 by Bishop Pudsey, but it was later converted into a castle by Bishop Anthony Bek in the 14th century. It has been the home of the Bishops of Durham for over 800 years, who in the past were virtually monarchs in their own kingdom. Over hundreds of years, the castle was expanded until in 1832 it became the official residence of the bishop and administrative centre for the diocese.

▲ **BISHOP AUCKLAND**
The Castle Gateway 1898 41459

The impressive Gothic gateway, crowned by a
turreted clock, was designed by Sir Thomas
Robinson around 1760 for Bishop Trevor.
The town of Bishop Auckland grew around the
castle and the extensive bishops' deer park with
its 18th-century deer house. It was in this park
that the English army was gathered together in
October 1346, before being marched to Durham to
do battle with the invading Scots at Nevilles Cross.

▶ **BISHOP AUCKLAND**
The Castle Chapel and the Reredos 1892
30711

This is St Peter's chapel, converted by John Cosin
and consecrated on St Peter's Day in 1665. It was
originally the grand banqueting hall for the manor
house built in the 12th century by Bishop Pudsey,
complete with buttery, wine cellar and minstrel
gallery. Bishop Joseph Lightfoot was responsible
for much of the restoration work in the 19th
century, including the addition of the beautifully
carved reredos; the lower portion consists of dark
Frosterley marble, and the upper of oak.

LAMBTON CASTLE *1892* 30718

During the 18th and 19th centuries, the coal industry dominated
the area, and the Lambton family rose to prominence through
wealth founded on coal. Ironically, shortly after being enlarged
and castellated in about 1833, the castle suffered severe structural
damage caused by mining subsidence. Local legend tells of the
Lambton Worm, which was slain by a bygone Lambton heir after
he took advice from a local witch. The witch then cursed him
because he refused to kill the first living thing he met after his
victory, and it is said that all subsequent Lambtons will die a
violent death because of this curse.

BARNARD CASTLE
The Bowes Museum 1914
67174

The Bowes Museum was designed and purpose-built as a public art gallery by the French architect Jules Pellechet on the outskirts of the historic town of Barnard Castle. The grand French chateau-style museum opened in 1892. It originated in a private foundation created between 1862 and 1875 by John Bowes, illegitimate son of the 10th Earl of Strathmore, and his Parisian actress wife, Josephine. They wanted to house the vast collection of works of art they had amassed from all corners of Europe so that people from all walks of life could see and enjoy them, but unfortunately they died before their dream was realised.

BARNARD CASTLE, *The Bowes Museum and the Gardens 1929* 82514

The museum is set in a large park with impressive formal gardens. The gardens, the chateau-style building, and the collection were all created from nothing over a period of fifteen years, always with the aim of public benefit.

BARNARD CASTLE
The Bowes Museum, the Balcony 1914
67179

The beautiful museum houses priceless works of art from all over Europe, and had the Queen Mother as its patron. John and Josephine Bowes, ancestors of the Queen Mother, built up their collection between 1862 and 1875. Much of their collection was made in Paris, and the museum building was designed to reflect this. The building is essentially a French museum on British soil.

BARNARD CASTLE, *The Bowes Museum, the Picture Gallery 1914* 67180

The museum has one of the most impressive collections in the country of pictures, ceramics, textiles, tapestries, clocks and costumes. It boasts a collection of European fine and decorative arts of the period 1400-1875, unrivalled in the North of England and outstanding in Britain. There is particular emphasis on the arts of France, including items from the Bowes' home in Paris.

HOUGHTON-LE-SPRING, *The Broadway c1955*
H225006

This view of the former mining town has changed little since
1955. The Red Lion is now an estate agents, and The White Lion
in the distance (left) is still there. People still wait for buses in
front of the church, although the queues are somewhat shorter
today! The white-sleeved policeman is on point duty at what was
once the main Durham to Sunderland road; a by-pass has made
the necessity for these duties long redundant.

HOUGHTON-LE-SPRING
The Parish Church c1959
H225008

The history of Houghton-le-Spring is centred round the attractive Norman church of St Michael and All Angels, within which we find the tomb of Bernard Gilpin (1517-1583), who was known as 'the Apostle of the North.' In 1557 Gilpin became the rector at Houghton-le-Spring, then one of the largest parishes in England. Despite his important status, Gilpin was a generous man who always had the interests of his parishioners at heart. On all Sundays between Michaelmas and Easter he declared his rectory an open house, and gave free dinners to all who visited, whether they were rich or poor.

SHERBURN, *The Village c1965* S289009

The village of Sherburn grew from a need to provide housing for miners and their families in the early 1800s. The village, known locally as 'The Hill', was thriving until the closure of the coal mine in 1965.

SHERBURN
The Parish Church
c1955 S289002

Designs for the new St Mary's church were completed in 1865; after some delays arising from modifications that were required to deal with underlying mine workings, the building was completed in 1872. The church cost £3,500 to build, and was consecrated on 28 May 1872.

WITTON GILBERT, *The War Memorial from the Woods c1955* W208002

Although it is near the church, it is still hard to understand why the war memorial was originally placed in a field on the outskirts of the village. This important monument has now been relocated close to the centre of the village, and it is now clearly visible and accessible.

LANGLEY PARK
General View c1965
L163037

Langley means 'long clearing', a woodland or forest clearing, and our photograph shows plainly how the sprawling Langley Park has spread across acres of cleared land. This former mining village has a wonderful blend of old and new, with modern housing on the outskirts and original stone buildings in the centre.

LANGLEY PARK, *Front Street c1955* L163021

The wide streets, stone buildings and the war memorial in the centre of Langley Park look much the same today. The village owes its present wide, open main streets' layout to the original fence lines of the dirt tracks that existed in 1856. These roads followed the exact lines of the present Quebec Street and Front Street, and the village was built around these.

COXHOE
The Cross-Roads c1955
C249001

The main A177 road south from Shincliffe leads to Coxhoe; it may follow the course of an old Roman road. The villages in this area are situated on the Magnesian limestone hills, which are typical of the east Durham countryside between Hartlepool and South Shields. The local limestone has been used in the past as building material, most notably to cement together the bricks of Durham Cathedral.

CROOK, *Hope Street c1955* C250019

Despite the enormous changes nationally in shopping habits, the
main street today still retains its straggle of small independent shops,
albeit on a steadily reducing scale, alongside the sprawling market
place and the two supermarkets.

CROOK, *Market Place c1955* C250017

Despite the fact that no pits have worked since 1960, many of the people who have lived in the town all their lives still regard Crook as a mining town. With the demise of the coal industry, the railway and the Co-operative Store also closed. The Co-operative Society in the north-east, with its renowned 'divi', was as much part of the fabric of the local community as the pits.

WILLINGTON, *High Street c1955* W247022

This typical High Street view could be of any village in the
north-east. This is the 1950s version of today's modern
superstore, where you can buy everything from ice cream to
petrol. Note the sign at the newsagents for Eldorado ice cream,
which was very popular at the time and one of the main
competitors of Walls. The Northern Echo newspaper is still one
of the most popular newspapers in the area.

WILLINGTON, *High Street c1955* W247016

This small town straddles the main route from Durham City to
Weardale, and was originally a settlement on an old Roman road.
Before 1840, Willington resembled many English farm villages in
the north-east - it was a collection of cottages and farmsteads. It
expanded in the 19th century as it became a pit village.

85

EASINGTON LANE, *The Memorial c1955* E86003

The war memorial and clock tower are still located in the
village High Street. Like so many other villages in this area,
Easington Lane rapidly developed into a large mining
community when coal breathed life into the area; sad to
say, it went into decline as the industry dwindled.

INDEX

NAMES OF SUBSCRIBERS

Edward Almond, Durham

David M. Anderson, Belmont, Durham City

Martin Anderson, Durham

John A. Ashworth, Durham

Graeme Banks, Durham

Alan Bennett, Durham

Alan Y. Black

Christopher Blacklock

Peter Blacklock

Mr J. M. Briggs

Mr S. A. Briggs

Frederick Brown, Durham

Dr & Mrs D. W. Burdon, Durham

Mrs S. A. Campbell & Mr N. Campbell

Brian Carpenter, Durham

K. Charlesworth, Durham City

Thomas H. Churnside

Doctor John Coates & Family, London

Thomas S. Colwell

Philip Cowell

Alice Crowe

Mr Brian Davidson, Durham City

Eric E. G. Davy, Durham

In memory of James Day

Janet Despres, Essex

Arthur Dews, Durham

Neil A. Dover, Durham

Ken & Cheryl Driver, Durham

Mrs L. Dunning

George Embleton, Durham

Brenda Emerson, Belmont, Durham

O. Farrey, Esh, Co. Durham

Mr & Mrs J. Gleghorn, St Annes on Sea

Robert J. H. Gregory & Nicola J. Gregory, Durham

Mr & Mrs Patrick Hagerty, Leeds

Mary R. Hawgood, Durham

S. & K. M. Hetherington

Mrs J. C. Hewison, Durham

Mrs L. Hope (Nanna)

Christopher J. Hugill

To Jack from Joy, Christmas 2003

Keith Johnson, Durham

Robert G. Johnson

N. Kell, Yorkshire

Dr Robert Kell

David Kelly, Durham

Francis C. Kirby

Frank Kirby

G. Kirby, Durham

Robert Kirby

R. Langton, Peterborough

Mr John David Leftley, Willington

Mrs M Leslie

Karina Lindsley, Durham

Frances & Derek Lorimer, Durham

Matthew G. Lynn

John McManners

Ann Moran, Durham

John J Moran, Durham

John A. Moreels, M.B.E., Durham

Nathan J. Murphy, Durham

Peter & Margaret Murray

Karen A. Napper, Durham

Charles Peter Nelson

Janet A. Nichols, Durham

Michael & Angela Orange, Durham

John Patterson, Carrville

Eric F. Patterson, Chavey Down

Howard L. Pattinson

Ian H. Pattinson

Brian Pine, Durham

Derek Pine, Durham

Geoffrey David Pledger

Malcolm & Frances Proud, Durham

M. Richardson, Durham

Tony Richmond

John Robert Robinson, Durham

Gary W. Rogerson, Leeds

Arneil G. Rutherford, Durham

John G. W. Scarr

Christine Scott, Durham

Alfred G. B. Shaw & Gail A. Shaw, Durham

F. L. Shevels, Newton Hall

Mrs O. M. Shield, Durham

Alexander Strachan, Newton Hall

Linda Thompson & David Toll, Briardene, Durham

Neil Thompson, Farnham

Robert B. Thompson, Durham

Christopher G. Tindale, Durham

Ronald Walters, Durham

Brenda Whatmore, Durham

Dr. R. D. Whatmore

Ian White, Newton Hall

FRITH PRODUCTS & SERVICES

Francis Frith would doubtless be pleased to know that the pioneering publishing venture he started in 1860 still continues today. Over a hundred and forty years later, The Francis Frith Collection continues in the same innovative tradition and is now one of the foremost publishers of vintage photographs in the world. Some of the current activities include:

Interior Decoration

Today Frith's photographs can be seen framed and as giant wall murals in thousands of pubs, restaurants, hotels, banks, retail stores and other public buildings throughout the country. In every case they enhance the unique local atmosphere of the places they depict and provide reminders of gentler days in an increasingly busy and frenetic world.

Product Promotions

Frith products are used by many major companies to promote the sales of their own products or to reinforce their own history and heritage. Frith promotions have been used by Hovis bread, Courage beers, Scots Porage Oats, Colman's mustard, Cadbury's foods, Mellow Birds coffee, Dunhill pipe tobacco, Guinness, and Bulmer's Cider.

Genealogy and Family History

As the interest in family history and roots grows world-wide, more and more people are turning to Frith's photographs of Great Britain for images of the towns, villages and streets where their ancestors lived; and, of course, photographs of the churches and chapels where their ancestors were christened, married and buried are an essential part of every genealogy tree and family album.

Frith Products

All Frith photographs are available Framed or just as Mounted Prints and Posters (size 23 x 16 inches). These may be ordered from the address below. From time to time other products - Address Books, Calendars, Table Mats, etc - are available.

The Internet

Already fifty thousand Frith photographs can be viewed and purchased on the internet through the Frith websites and a myriad of partner sites.

For more detailed information on Frith companies and products, look at these sites:

www.francisfrith.co.uk
www.francisfrith.com
(for North American visitors)

See the complete list of Frith Books at:

www.francisfrith.co.uk

This web site is regularly updated with the latest list of publications from the Frith Book Company. If you wish to buy books relating to another part of the country that your local bookshop does not stock, you may purchase on-line.

For further information, trade, or author enquiries please contact us at the address below:
The Francis Frith Collection, Frith's Barn, Teffont, Salisbury, Wiltshire, England SP3 5QP.
Tel: +44 (0)1722 716 376 Fax: +44 (0)1722 716 881 Email: sales@francisfrith.co.uk

See Frith books on the internet at www.francisfrith.co.uk

FREE MOUNTED PRINT

Mounted Print
Overall size 14 x 11 inches

Fill in and cut out this voucher and return
it with your remittance for £2.25 (to cover postage and handling). Offer valid for delivery to UK addresses only.

Choose any photograph included in this book.
Your SEPIA print will be A4 in size. It will be mounted in a cream mount with a burgundy rule line (overall size 14 x 11 inches).

Order additional Mounted Prints
at HALF PRICE (only £7.49 each*)
If you would like to order more Frith prints from this book, possibly as gifts for friends and family, you can buy them at half price (with no additional postage and handling costs).

Have your Mounted Prints framed
For an extra £14.95 per print* you can have your mounted print(s) framed in an elegant polished wood and gilt moulding, overall size 16 x 13 inches (no additional postage and handling required).

---

* IMPORTANT!

These special prices are only available if you order at the same time as you order your free mounted print. You must use the ORIGINAL VOUCHER on this page (no copies permitted). We can only despatch to one address.

Send completed Voucher form to:
The Francis Frith Collection, Frith's Barn, Teffont, Salisbury, Wiltshire SP3 5QP

CHOOSE ANY IMAGE FROM THIS BOOK

Voucher for **FREE** and Reduced Price Frith Prints

Please do not photocopy this voucher. Only the original is valid, so please fill it in, cut it out and return it to us with your order.

Picture ref no	Page no	Qty	Mounted @ £7.49	Framed + £14.95	Total Cost
		1	Free of charge*	£	£
			£7.49	£	£
			£7.49	£	£
			£7.49	£	£
			£7.49	£	£
			£7.49	£	£

Please allow 28 days for delivery

* Post & handling (UK)	£2.25
Total Order Cost	£

Title of this book . . . .

I enclose a cheque/postal order for £ . . . .
made payable to 'The Francis Frith Collection'

OR please debit my Mastercard / Visa / Switch / Amex card
(credit cards please on all overseas orders), details below

Card Number

Issue No (Switch only)   Valid from (Amex/Switch)

Expires   Signature

Name   Mr/Mrs/Ms . . . .
Address . . . .
. . . .
. . . .
. . . . Postcode . . . .
Daytime Tel No . . . .
Email . . . .

Valid to 31/12/05

Free Print – see overleaf

Would you like to find out more about Francis Frith?

We have recently recruited some entertaining speakers who are happy to visit local groups, clubs and societies to give an illustrated talk documenting Frith's travels and photographs. If you are a member of such a group and are interested in hosting a presentation, we would love to hear from you.

Our speakers bring with them a small selection of our local town and county books, together with sample prints. They are happy to take orders. A small proportion of the order value is donated to the group who have hosted the presentation. The talks are therefore an excellent way of fundraising for small groups and societies.

Can you help us with information about any of the Frith photographs in this book?

We are gradually compiling an historical record for each of the photographs in the Frith archive. It is always fascinating to find out the names of the people shown in the pictures, as well as insights into the shops, buildings and other features depicted.

If you recognize anyone in the photographs in this book, or if you have information not already included in the author's caption, do let us know. We would love to hear from you, and will try to publish it in future books or articles.

Our production team

Frith books are produced by a small dedicated team at offices in the converted Grade II listed 18th-century barn at Teffont near Salisbury, illustrated above. Most have worked with the Frith Collection for many years. All have in common one quality: they have a passion for the Frith Collection. The team is constantly expanding, but currently includes:

Jason Buck, John Buck, Douglas Mitchell-Burns, Ruth Butler, Heather Crisp, Isobel Hall, Julian Hight, Peter Horne, James Kinnear, Karen Kinnear, Tina Leary, David Marsh, Sue Molloy, Kate Rotondetto, Dean Scource, Eliza Sackett, Terence Sackett, Sandra Sampson, Adrian Sanders, Sandra Sanger, Julia Skinner, Lewis Taylor, Shelley Tolcher and Lorraine Tuck.